The Mission of Addition

To my brother Mike,
the numbers guy in our family
—B.P.C.

Addition:
Combining two
or more numbers
to come up
with their total

The Mission of Addition

by Brian P. Cleary
illustrated by Brian Gable

M MILLBROOK PRESS / MINNEAPOLIS

Adding

is growing the total of things,

6 yellow buses were parked in a line.

Along came 4 more, and that made 13.

To **add** is to make bigger
the total number of
whatever you are counting up,

like baseballs in a glove.

7 batters
plus 2 more
make 9 when they are added.

The number just gets bigger
with each one who has batted.

No amount gets smaller
When you're Working
in **addition**.

The numbers climb
from low to high,
'cause that's
addition's mission!

The Johnsons had **1** babysitter.
Gretchen was her name.

She cried "**Help!**"

So, number **2**,
Miss Higgenbottom,
came.

So far,
this made **4** who tried
to keep them all in line.

5th was
Caitlyn MacNamee,

and 6th was Mr. Lee,
and 1 more
———
totaled 10 in all
to watch that crew of 3.

You see,
to **add** means to **increase**.
It's a way of showing more,

whether counting babysitters

or bread crusts on the floor.

"Plus" can be used
just like "**and**."
It helps us
when we count,

combining all the numbers
till we get
the full amount.

"Equals" can be used like "is,"
or "totals,"
even "makes."

It doesn't matter if you're adding friends or birthday cakes.

So, if a hen lays 7 eggs
plus 3,
plus 4,
plus 10,
the total equals 24...

and **1** exhausted hen!

In counting the musicians
in the marching band at school,
you add up all the players
from each group.

Just look, it's cool!

9 are playing trumpet,
plus 3 are on trombone.
2 more jam on flügelhorn
and 6 on saxophone.

When you add 8
bass drummers in,
that equals 28.

So, when it comes to counting, don't worry, fret, or fuss.

You'll find that knowing
how to **add**

is very much a **plus**!

So, what is addition?

Do you know?

Millbrook Press
A division of Lerner Publishing Group
241 First Avenue North
Minneapolis, MN 55401 USA

Website address: www.lernerbooks.com

Library of Congress Cataloging-in-Publication Data

Cleary, Brian P., 1959—
    The mission of addition / by Brian P. Cleary ; illustrated by Brian Gable.
        p.   cm.—(Math is categorical)
    ISBN-13: 978-1-57505-859-7 (lib. bdg. : alk. paper)
    ISBN-10: 1-57505-859-6 (lib. bdg. : alk. paper)
    1. Arithmetic—Study and teaching (Primary) 2. Addition—Study and
teaching (Primary) I. Gable, Brian, 1949— ill. II. Title.
QA135.6.C54 2005
513.2'11—dc22   2004031105

Manufactured in the United States of America
1 2 3 4 5 6 — JR — 10 09 08 07 06 05